Building an Army

Children's Military & War History Books

BABY PROFESSOR

EDUCATION KIDS

Speedy Publishing LLC
40 E. Main St. #1156
Newark, DE 19711
www.speedypublishing.com

Throughout history, the nation with the strongest, most effective army almost always dominates and rules over those that are weaker.

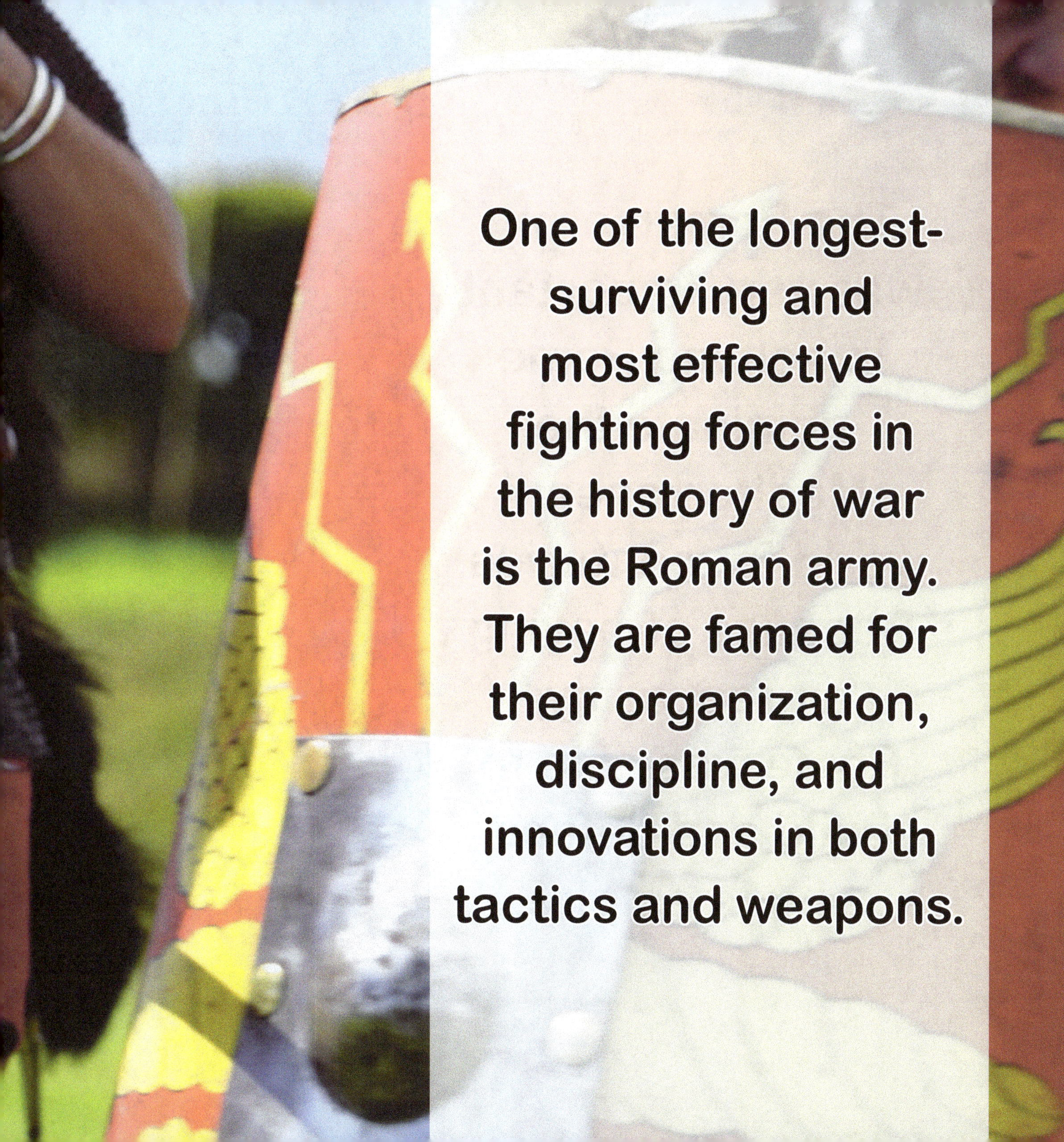

One of the longest-surviving and most effective fighting forces in the history of war is the Roman army. They are famed for their organization, discipline, and innovations in both tactics and weapons.

The Roman army was very important in helping Rome dominate the Mediterranean world for centuries. Because of having a great army, Rome was able to build and defend a huge empire.

The Roman Empire

in 117 AD, at its greatest extent

Romulus, the one believed to be the founder of Rome, is said to have created the legionary forces. The early Roman army used a form of civil militia, recruiting citizens depending on social standing and the immediate need. The year-round, full-time army was very small.

Around 580-530 BCE, King Servius Tullius introduced six classes of wealth to classify the citizens of Rome. The lowest class had no property and they were excluded from joining the military, while the highest class, the equites, formed the cavalry.

Around 150-120 BCE, the Roman army had a structure known as the Manipular Legion, in which each legion was composed of smaller units of 120-160 men called maniples (Latin for handfuls).

All armies want to
be paid. Payments
do not have to
be in the form of
money. Soldiers
will accept land,
recognition,
attention,
special training,
goodwill, and
other intangible
benefits.

LEG VI
LEG VI
LEG VI
LEG VI

Armies like field
assignments.
They want
a mission
with clear
parameters, field
intelligence, and
mission briefings.
They would
like to know
that someone
is looking
out for them
and counting
on them.

Here are a few
common practices
to build an army:

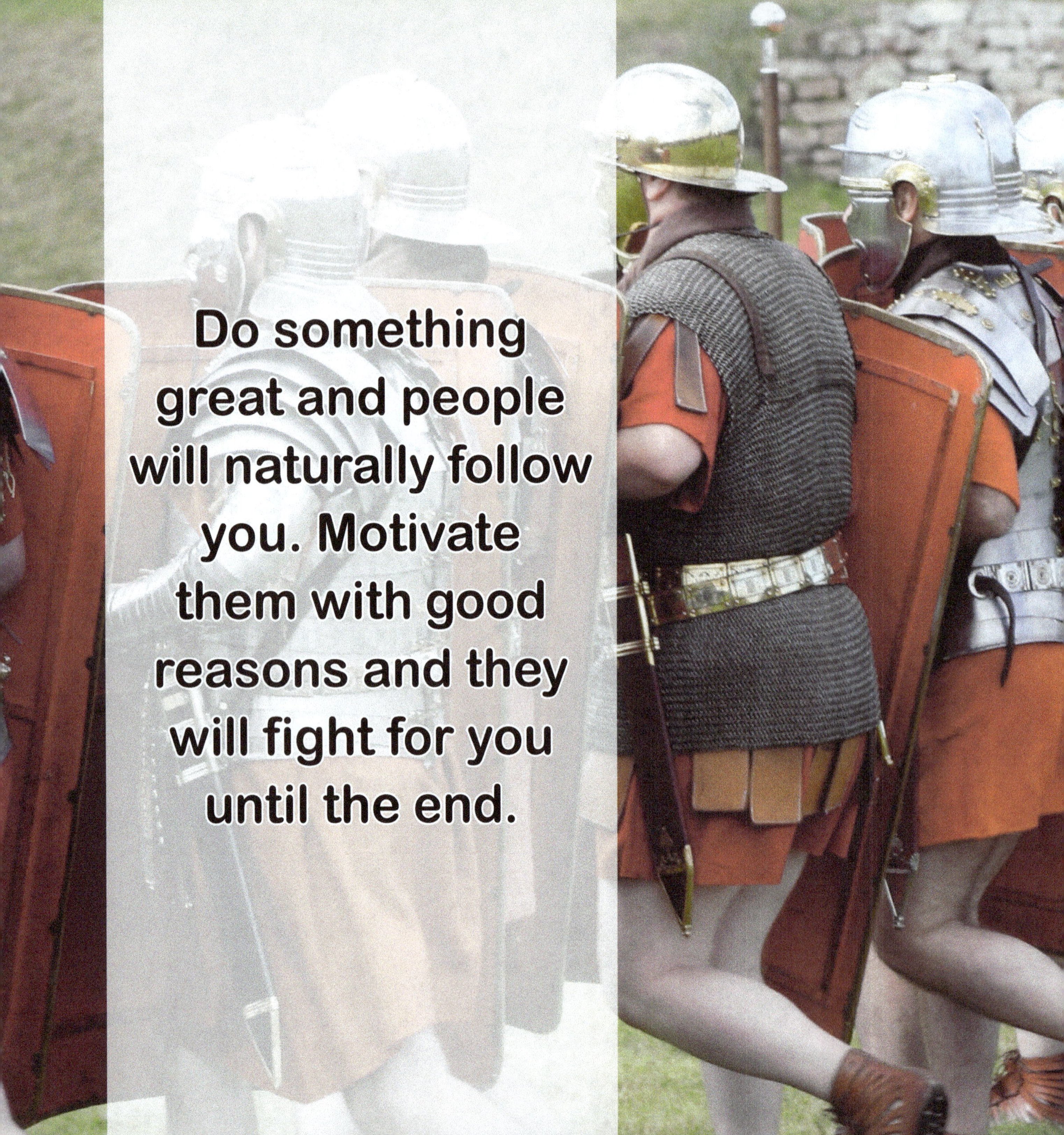
Do something
great and people
will naturally follow
you. Motivate
them with good
reasons and they
will fight for you
until the end.

LEG VI
LEG VI
LEG VI

Look at the people closest to you who are willing to help you in your cause. They will likely help you in recruiting people.

Announce your plans so people will know why the army is needed, and what its success will look like. Set up a sign-up list for people who are willing to be part of your army.

In military history, many of those who were recruited were promised land to own when they finished their military service. Others also join the army to protect what they already have.

Still others join
to prove to their
family and friends
that they love
their country
and are brave
enough to defend
their cause even
if that means
losing their lives.

Coming off
victorious from war
does not always
mean happiness.
At the end of World
War I, the American
foreign policy
can be summed
up in two words:
Never again.

Many Americans felt that the Great War was also a great mistake and they hoped that it was the war to end all the wars. If war was obsolete, then there would be no need for strong military forces.

But war has not ended yet. We see that almost all nations have their own military forces to defend their country from possible threats of invasion.

There is much
more to know
about building an
army. Research
and become
wise before you
declare any wars!

Visit
BABY PROFESSOR
EDUCATION KIDS
www.BabyProfessorBooks.com
to download Free Baby Professor eBooks
and view our catalog of new and exciting
Children's Books